COMPARATIVE FONTS

A comparison of fonts available in Microsoft Word

'Little Lord Fontleroy'

Comparative Fonts

Danzmark Productions, Houston, Texas, Publisher

Special thanks to Mr. Ben Young, 'Shooters Station' gun range, gentleman extraordinary, for proofing this book.

ISBN 978-1-312-86277-7

Comparative Fonts

Table of Contents

Comparative Fonts

Comparative Fonts

Preface & Commentary

Written in 'Times New Roman' -12 Font

Desktop publishing authors have a choice of several 100 to reportedly 1001 fonts in existence; per Mr. Google. This book presents a series of fonts selected from those available in Microsoft Word 2007. The book's purpose is to give the writer a handy place to compare fonts rather than 'trial-and-error' tasking in the manuscript. Chosing a font is the writer's prerogative, but ideally the font should complement the text topic.

For comparison purposes, the fonts are each used in printing the same paragraph on successive pages; the paragraph is the data page on the novel **'Little Lord Fauntleroy'**; the first children's novel written by English playwright and author Frances Hodgson Burnett.

With apologies to Frances Hodgson Burnett, the similarity between **'Font'**, **'Fontleroy'** and **'Fauntleroy'** is sufficient excuse to utilize the Fauntleroy paragraph to illustrate each font example.

Writers can select from numerous font sizes and, additionally, apply **bold** and *italics*. Font size 11 is about the smallest suitable for text; Font size 12 is ideal for text; and font size 14 is about maximum for text.

Comparative Fonts

This book starts with two popular fonts for general text writing: 'Times New Roman' and '**Franklin Gothic Medium**', and goes on in alphabetical order to include many specialized and novelty fonts.

Page composition containing illustrations is a reason to vary the fonts and font size. Typically, the illustrations are sized to the maximum and the text adapted likewise to achieve a complete topic page without **'spillover'** onto the following page. It is good practice to end each page with a complete sentence, and start the next page with a complete sentence; this may leave some minor blank space on the first page, which is literarily acceptable. All fonts in any related text of a book should strive to be in identical size.. Some same-size fonts are more compact than others and this assists in this compilation process.

Utilizing a different same size font on quotes and words that can be emphasized adds to the text clarity and appearance. Direct quotes with identified author should be in **"quotation"** marks:

George Washington said **"I cannot tell a lie – I chopped the cherry tree down."**

Words that would be just better emphasized should have 'single marks'

Comparative Fonts

John read 'The Pilgrims Progress' in grammar school. Note switch from Times New Roman 12 to Franklin Gothic Medium 12.

Text on a scientific subject or directions on how to do something are appropriate in fonts such as Arial, Cambria or Veranda. The following text is Arial 12:

"In much specialist writing, including linguistics, philosophy, and theology, terms with particular meanings that are unique to that subject are often enclosed in single quotation marks:

The inner margins of a book are called the 'gutter.'

Many people do not realize that 'cultivar' is synonymous with 'clone.'

An example of an apple is 'Jonathon,' of a grape, 'Chardonnay,' and of the Gallica rose, 'Rosa Munda'."

The use of single quotation marks is standard practice in Great Britain, but Americans typically use double quotation marks on everything. However, the language is 'English', so English usage properly prevails; not to mention makes more sense.

Comparative Fonts

Franklin Gothic Medium size 12 is larger than Times New Roman size 12. **Using size 11 instead of size 12 Franklin Gothic Medium is a space-saving option that is indiscernible by the average reader.**

Samuel Clemens wrote under the pen name **'Mark Twain'**; here **'Mark Twain' is in Franklin Gothic Medium size 12.**

Samuel Clemens wrote under the pen name **'Mark Twain'**; here **'Mark Twain'** is in Franklin Gothic Medium size 11.

A consideration in font selection is delineating a long text by someone else from text by the writer. For example, 'Lincoln's **Gettysburg Address**' would look better in **Arial** if the writer's text was Times New Roman.

In comparing the fonts in this book, the reader can measure up to the paragraph from the bottom of the page to note just how much space that paragraph in that font took.

To add a commercial, this book was printed by LuLu.com, with expert free computer compiling, excellent printing results, and **'Print-on-Demand' with only the cost of buying the book.**

Daniel Warvelle Harbaugh, February 2015

Comparative Fonts

Times New Roman   - 12

Little Lord Fauntleroy is the first children's novel written by English playwright and author Frances Hodgson Burnett. It was originally published as a serial in the *St. Nicholas Magazine* between November 1885 and October 1886, then as a book by Scribner's in 1886. [The accompanying illustrations by Reginald Birch set fashion trends and *Little Lord Fauntleroy* also set a precedent in copyright law when in 1888 its author won a lawsuit against E. V. Seebohm over the rights to theatrical adaptations of the work.

Aa Bb Cc Dd Ee Ff Gg Hh Ii Jj Kk Ll Mm Nn Oo Pp Qq Rr Ss Tt Uu Vv Ww Xx Yy Zz

Comparative Fonts

Franklin Gothic Medium   - 12

Little Lord Fauntleroy is the first children's novel written by English playwright and author Frances Hodgson Burnett. It was originally published as a serial in the *St. Nicholas Magazine* between November 1885 and October 1886, then as a book by Scribner's in 1886. [The accompanying illustrations by Reginald Birch set fashion trends and *Little Lord Fauntleroy* also set a precedent in copyright law when in 1888 its author won a lawsuit against E. V. Seebohm over the rights to theatrical adaptations of the work.

Aa Bb Cc Dd Ee Ff Gg Hh Ii Jj Kk Ll Mm Nn Oo Pp Qq Rr Ss Tt Uu Vv Ww Xx Yy Zz

Franklin Gothic Medium   - 11

Little Lord Fauntleroy is the first children's novel written by English playwright and author Frances Hodgson Burnett. It was originally published as a serial in the *St. Nicholas Magazine* between November 1885 and October 1886, then as a book by Scribner's in 1886. [The accompanying illustrations by Reginald Birch set fashion trends and *Little Lord Fauntleroy* also set a precedent in copyright law when in 1888 its author won a lawsuit against E. V. Seebohm over the rights to theatrical adaptations of the work.

Microsoft Sans Serif - 12

Little Lord Fauntleroy is the first children's novel
written by English playwright and author Frances
Hodgson Burnett. It was originally published as a
serial in the *St. Nicholas Magazine* between
November 1885 and October 1886, then as a book
by Scribner's in 1886. The accompanying
illustrations by Reginald Birch set fashion trends
and *Little Lord Fauntleroy* also set a precedent in
copyright law when in 1888 its author won a lawsuit
against E. V. Seebohm over the rights to theatrical
adaptations of the work.

Aa Bb Cc Dd Ee Ff Gg Hh Ii Jj Kk Ll Mm Nn Oo Pp
Qq Rr Ss Tt Uu Vv Ww Xx Yy Zz

Microsoft has nine fonts. Assuming Microsoft is on the
cutting edge of the font business, their fonts are to be
considered.

ALGERIAN - 12

LITTLE LORD FAUNTLEROY IS THE FIRST CHILDREN'S NOVEL WRITTEN BY ENGLISH PLAYWRIGHT AND AUTHOR FRANCES HODGSON BURNETT. IT WAS ORIGINALLY PUBLISHED AS A SERIAL IN THE *ST. NICHOLAS MAGAZINE* BETWEEN NOVEMBER 1885 AND OCTOBER 1886, THEN AS A BOOK BY SCRIBNER'S IN 1886. THE ACCOMPANYING ILLUSTRATIONS BY REGINALD BIRCH SET FASHION TRENDS AND *LITTLE LORD FAUNTLEROY* ALSO SET A PRECEDENT IN COPYRIGHT LAW WHEN IN 1888 ITS AUTHOR WON A LAWSUIT AGAINST E. V. SEEBOHM OVER THE RIGHTS TO THEATRICAL ADAPTATIONS OF THE WORK.

AA BB CC DD EE FF GG HH II JJ KK LL MM NN OO PP QQ RR SS TT UU VV WW XX YY ZZ

Comparative Fonts

Arial   - 12

Little Lord Fauntleroy is the first children's novel written by English playwright and author Frances Hodgson Burnett. It was originally published as a serial in the *St. Nicholas Magazine* between November 1885 and October 1886, then as a book by Scribner's in 1886. The accompanying illustrations by Reginald Birch set fashion trends and *Little Lord Fauntleroy* also set a precedent in copyright law when in 1888 its author won a lawsuit against E. V. Seebohm over the rights to theatrical adaptations of the work.

Aa Bb Cc Dd Ee Ff Gg Hh Ii Jj Kk Ll Mm Nn Oo Pp Qq Rr Ss Tt Uu Vv Ww Xx Yy Zz

Comparative Fonts

Arial Narrow - 12

Little Lord Fauntleroy is the first children's novel written by English playwright and author Frances Hodgson Burnett. It was originally published as a serial in the *St. Nicholas Magazine* between November 1885 and October 1886, then as a book by Scribner's in 1886. The accompanying illustrations by Reginald Birch set fashion trends and *Little Lord Fauntleroy* also set a precedent in copyright law when in 1888 its author won a lawsuit against E. V. Seebohm over the rights to theatrical adaptations of the work.

Aa Bb Cc Dd Ee Ff Gg Hh Ii Jj Kk Ll Mm Nn Oo Pp Qq Rr Ss Tt Uu Vv Ww Xx Yy

Arial Rounded MT Bold - 12

Little Lord Fauntleroy is the first children's novel written by English playwright and author Frances Hodgson Burnett. It was originally published as a serial in the *St. Nicholas Magazine* between November 1885 and October 1886, then as a book by Scribner's in 1886. [The accompanying illustrations by Reginald Birch set fashion trends and *Little Lord Fauntleroy* also set a precedent in copyright law when in 1888 its author won a lawsuit against E. V. Seebohm over the rights to theatrical adaptations of the work.

Aa Bb Cc Dd Ee Ff Gg Hh Ii Jj Kk Ll Mm Nn Oo Pp Qq Rr Ss Tt Uu Vv Ww Xx Yy Zz

Comparative Fonts

Arial Unicode MS -12

Little Lord Fauntleroy is the first children's novel written by English playwright and author Frances Hodgson Burnett. It was originally published as a serial in the *St. Nicholas Magazine* between November 1885 and October 1886, then as a book by Scribner's in 1886. [The accompanying illustrations by Reginald Birch set fashion trends and *Little Lord Fauntleroy* also set a precedent in copyright law when in 1888 its author won a lawsuit against E. V. Seebohm over the rights to theatrical adaptations of the work.

Aa Bb Cc Dd Ee Ff Gg Hh Ii Jj Kk Ll Mm Nn Oo Pp Qq Rr Ss Tt Uu Vv Ww Xx Yy Zz

Comparative Fonts

Baskerville Old Face - 12

Little Lord Fauntleroy is the first children's novel written by English playwright and author Frances Hodgson Burnett. It was originally published as a serial in the *St. Nicholas Magazine* between November 1885 and October 1886, then as a book by Scribner's in 1886. The accompanying illustrations by Reginald Birch set fashion trends and *Little Lord Fauntleroy* also set a precedent in copyright law when in 1888 its author won a lawsuit against E. V. Seebohm over the rights to theatrical adaptations of the work.

Aa Bb Cc Dd Ee Ff Gg Hh Ii Jj Kk Ll Mm Nn Oo Pp Qq Rr Ss Tt Uu Vv Ww Xx Yy Zz

Comparative Fonts

Batang – 12

Little Lord Fauntleroy is the first children's novel written by English playwright and author Frances Hodgson Burnett. It was originally published as a serial in the *St. Nicholas Magazine* between November 1885 and October 1886, then as a book by Scribner's in 1886. [The accompanying illustrations by Reginald Birch set fashion trends and *Little Lord Fauntleroy* also set a precedent in copyright law when in 1888 its author won a lawsuit against E. V. Seebohm over the rights to theatrical adaptations of the work.

Aa Bb Cc Dd Ee Ff Gg Hh Ii Jj Kk Ll Mm Nn Oo Pp Qq Rr Ss Tt Uu Vv Ww Xx Yy Zz

Comparative Fonts

Bell MT   - 12

Little Lord Fauntleroy is the first children's novel written by English playwright and author Frances Hodgson Burnett. It was originally published as a serial in the *St. Nicholas Magazine* between November 1885 and October 1886, then as a book by Scribner's in 1886. ⌐The accompanying illustrations by Reginald Birch set fashion trends and *Little Lord Fauntleroy* also set a precedent in copyright law when in 1888 its author won a lawsuit against E. V. Seebohm over the rights to theatrical adaptations of the work.

Aa Bb Cc Dd Ee Ff Gg Hh Ii Jj Kk Ll Mm Nn Oo Pp Qq Rr Ss Tt Uu Vv Ww Xx Yy Zz

Comparative Fonts

Berlin Sans FB - 12

Little Lord Fauntleroy is the first children's novel written by English playwright and author Frances Hodgson Burnett. It was originally published as a serial in the *St. Nicholas Magazine* between November 1885 and October 1886, then as a book by Scribner's in 1886. [The accompanying illustrations by Reginald Birch set fashion trends and *Little Lord Fauntleroy* also set a precedent in copyright law when in 1888 its author won a lawsuit against E. V. Seebohm over the rights to theatrical adaptations of the work.

Aa Bb Cc Dd Ee Ff Gg Hh Ii Jj Kk Ll Mm Nn Oo Pp Qq Rr Ss Tt Uu Vv Ww Xx Yy Zz

Bodoni MT   - 12

Little Lord Fauntleroy is the first children's novel written by English playwright and author Frances Hodgson Burnett. It was originally published as a serial in the *St. Nicholas Magazine* between November 1885 and October 1886, then as a book by Scribner's in 1886. ᛌThe accompanying illustrations by Reginald Birch set fashion trends and *Little Lord Fauntleroy* also set a precedent in copyright law when in 1888 its author won a lawsuit against E. V. Seebohm over the rights to theatrical adaptations of the work.

Aa Bb Cc Dd Ee Ff Gg Hh Ii Jj Kk Ll Mm Nn Oo Pp Qq Rr Ss Tt Uu Vv Ww Xx YyZz

Comparative Fonts

Book Antiqua - 12

Little Lord Fauntleroy is the first children's novel written by English playwright and author Frances Hodgson Burnett. It was originally published as a serial in the *St. Nicholas Magazine* between November 1885 and October 1886, then as a book by Scribner's in 1886. The accompanying illustrations by Reginald Birch set fashion trends and *Little Lord Fauntleroy* also set a precedent in copyright law when in 1888 its author won a lawsuit against E. V. Seebohm over the rights to theatrical adaptations of the work.

Aa Bb Cc Dd Ee Ff Gg Hh Ii Jj Kk Ll Mm Nn Oo Pp Qq Rr Ss Tt Uu Vv Ww Xx Yy Zz

Britannic Bold - 12

Little Lord Fauntleroy is the first children's novel written by English playwright and author Frances Hodgson Burnett. It was originally published as a serial in the *St. Nicholas Magazine* between November 1885 and October 1886, then as a book by Scribner's in 1886. ¹The accompanying illustrations by Reginald Birch set fashion trends and *Little Lord Fauntleroy* also set a precedent in copyright law when in 1888 its author won a lawsuit against E. V. Seebohm over the rights to theatrical adaptations of the work.

Aa Bb Cc Dd Ee Ff Gg Hh Ii Jj Kk Ll Mm Nn Oo Pp Qq Rr Ss Tt Uu Vv Ww Xx Yy Zz

Broadway - 12

Little Lord Fauntleroy is the first children's novel written by English playwright and author Frances Hodgson Burnett. It was originally published as a serial in the *St. Nicholas Magazine* between November 1885 and October 1886, then as a book by Scribner's in 1886. The accompanying illustrations by Reginald Birch set fashion trends and *Little Lord Fauntleroy* also set a precedent in copyright law when in 1888 its author won a lawsuit against E. V. Seebohm over the rights to theatrical adaptations of the work.

Aa Bb Cc Dd Ee Ff Gg Hh Ii Jj Kk Ll Mm Nn Oo Pp Qq Rr Ss Tt Uu Vv Ww Xx Yy Zz

Comparative Fonts

Calibri - 12

Little Lord Fauntleroy is the first children's novel written by English playwright and author Frances Hodgson Burnett. It was originally published as a serial in the *St. Nicholas Magazine* between November 1885 and October 1886, then as a book by Scribner's in 1886. [The accompanying illustrations by Reginald Birch set fashion trends and *Little Lord Fauntleroy* also set a precedent in copyright law when in 1888 its author won a lawsuit against E. V. Seebohm over the rights to theatrical adaptations of the work.

Aa Bb Cc Dd Ee Ff Gg Hh Ii Jj Kk Ll Mm Nn Oo Pp Qq Rr Ss Tt Uu Vv Ww Xx Yy Zz

Californian FB - 12

Little Lord Fauntleroy is the first children's novel written by English playwright and author Frances Hodgson Burnett. It was originally published as a serial in the *St. Nicholas Magazine* between November 1885 and October 1886, then as a book by Scribner's in 1886. [The accompanying illustrations by Reginald Birch set fashion trends and *Little Lord Fauntleroy* also set a precedent in copyright law when in 1888 its author won a lawsuit against E. V. Seebohm over the rights to theatrical adaptations of the work.

Aa Bb Cc Dd Ee Ff Gg Hh Ii Jj Kk Ll Mm Nn Oo Pp Qq Rr Ss Tt Uu Vv Ww Xx Yy Zz

Calisto MT   - 12

Little Lord Fauntleroy is the first children's novel
written by English playwright and author Frances
Hodgson Burnett. It was originally published as a
serial in the *St. Nicholas Magazine* between November
1885 and October 1886, then as a book by Scribner's
in 1886. [The accompanying illustrations by Reginald
Birch set fashion trends and *Little Lord Fauntleroy* also
set a precedent in copyright law when in 1888 its
author won a lawsuit against E. V. Seebohm over the
rights to theatrical adaptations of the work.

Aa Bb Cc Dd Ee Ff Gg Hh Ii Jj Kk Ll Mm Nn Oo Pp
Qq Rr Ss Tt Uu Vv Ww Xx Yy Zz

Comparative Fonts

Cambria   - 12

Little Lord Fauntleroy is the first children's novel written by English playwright and author Frances Hodgson Burnett. It was originally published as a serial in the *St. Nicholas Magazine* between November 1885 and October 1886, then as a book by Scribner's in 1886. ⌐The accompanying illustrations by Reginald Birch set fashion trends and *Little Lord Fauntleroy* also set a precedent in copyright law when in 1888 its author won a lawsuit against E. V. Seebohm over the rights to theatrical adaptations of the work.

Aa Bb Cc Dd Ee Ff Gg Hh Ii Jj Kk Ll Mm Nn Oo Pp Qq Rr Ss Tt Uu Vv Ww Xx Yy Zz

Comparative Fonts

Cambria Math - 12

Little Lord Fauntleroy is the first children's novel written by English playwright and author Frances Hodgson Burnett. It was originally published as a serial in the *St. Nicholas Magazine* between November 1885 and October 1886, then as a book by Scribner's in 1886. ⌐The accompanying illustrations by Reginald Birch set fashion trends and *Little Lord Fauntleroy* also set a precedent in copyright law when in 1888 its author won a lawsuit against E. V. Seebohm over the rights to theatrical adaptations of the work.

Aa Bb Cc Dd Ee Ff Gg Hh Ii Jj Kk Ll Mm Nn Oo Pp Qq Rr Ss Tt Uu Vv Ww Xx Yy

Comparative Fonts

Candara - 12

Little Lord Fauntleroy is the first children's novel written by English playwright and author Frances Hodgson Burnett. It was originally published as a serial in the *St. Nicholas Magazine* between November 1885 and October 1886, then as a book by Scribner's in 1886. ⌐The accompanying illustrations by Reginald Birch set fashion trends and *Little Lord Fauntleroy* also set a precedent in copyright law when in 1888 its author won a lawsuit against E. V. Seebohm over the rights to theatrical adaptations of the work.

Aa Bb Cc Dd Ee Ff Gg Hh Ii Jj Kk Ll Mm Nn Oo Pp Qq Rr Ss Tt Uu Vv Ww Xx Yy

Comparative Fonts

Centaur - 12

Little Lord Fauntleroy is the first children's novel written by English playwright and author Frances Hodgson Burnett. It was originally published as a serial in the *St. Nicholas Magazine* between November 1885 and October 1886, then as a book by Scribner's in 1886. The accompanying illustrations by Reginald Birch set fashion trends and *Little Lord Fauntleroy* also set a precedent in copyright law when in 1888 its author won a lawsuit against E. V. Seebohm over the rights to theatrical adaptations of the work.

Aa Bb Cc Dd Ee Ff Gg Hh Ii Jj Kk Ll Mm Nn Oo Pp Qq Rr Ss Tt Uu Vv Ww Xx Yy Zz

Comparative Fonts

Century Gothic   - 12

Little Lord Fauntleroy is the first children's novel written by English playwright and author Frances Hodgson Burnett. It was originally published as a serial in the *St. Nicholas Magazine* between November 1885 and October 1886, then as a book by Scribner's in 1886. The accompanying illustrations by Reginald Birch set fashion trends and *Little Lord Fauntleroy* also set a precedent in copyright law when in 1888 its author won a lawsuit against E. V. Seebohm over the rights to theatrical adaptations of the work.

Aa Bb Cc Dd Ee Ff Gg Hh Ii Jj Kk Ll Mm Nn Oo Pp Qq Rr Ss Tt Uu Vv Ww Xx Yy Zz

Comparative Fonts

Century Schoolbook   - 12

Little Lord Fauntleroy is the first children's novel written by English playwright and author Frances Hodgson Burnett. It was originally published as a serial in the *St. Nicholas Magazine* between November 1885 and October 1886, then as a book by Scribner's in 1886. The accompanying illustrations by Reginald Birch set fashion trends and *Little Lord Fauntleroy* also set a precedent in copyright law when in 1888 its author won a lawsuit against E. V. Seebohm over the rights to theatrical adaptations of the work.

Aa Bb Cc Dd Ee Ff Gg Hh Ii Jj Kk Ll Mm Nn Oo Pp Qq Rr Ss Tt Uu Vv Ww Xx Yy Zz

Comic Sans MS   - 12

Little Lord Fauntleroy is the first children's novel written by English playwright and author Frances Hodgson Burnett. It was originally published as a serial in the *St. Nicholas Magazine* between November 1885 and October 1886, then as a book by Scribner's in 1886. [The accompanying illustrations by Reginald Birch set fashion trends and *Little Lord Fauntleroy* also set a precedent in copyright law when in 1888 its author won a lawsuit against E. V. Seebohm over the rights to theatrical adaptations of the work.

Aa Bb Cc Dd Ee Ff Gg Hh Ii Jj Kk Ll Mm Nn Oo Pp Qq Rr Ss Tt Uu Vv Ww Xx Yy Zz

Comparative Fonts

David - 12

Little Lord Fauntleroy is the first children's novel written by English playwright and author Frances Hodgson Burnett. It was originally published as a serial in the *St. Nicholas Magazine* between November 1885 and October 1886, then as a book by Scribner's in 1886. [The accompanying illustrations by Reginald Birch set fashion trends and *Little Lord Fauntleroy* also set a precedent in copyright law when in 1888 its author won a lawsuit against E. V. Seebohm over the rights to theatrical adaptations of the work.

Aa Bb Cc Dd Ee Ff Gg Hh Ii Jj Kk Ll Mm Nn Oo Pp Qq Rr Ss Tt Uu Vv Ww Xx Yy Zz

DejaVu Sans - 12

Little Lord Fauntleroy is the first children's novel written by English playwright and author Frances Hodgson Burnett. It was originally published as a serial in the *St. Nicholas Magazine* between November 1885 and October 1886, then as a book by Scribner's in 1886. [The accompanying illustrations by Reginald Birch set fashion trends and *Little Lord Fauntleroy* also set a precedent in copyright law when in 1888 its author won a lawsuit against E. V. Seebohm over the rights to theatrical adaptations of the work.

Aa Bb Cc Dd Ee Ff Gg Hh Ii Jj Kk Ll Mm Nn Oo Pp Qq Rr Ss Tt Uu Vv Ww Xx Yy Zz

DejaVu Sans Condense -12

Little Lord Fauntleroy is the first children's novel written by English playwright and author Frances Hodgson Burnett. It was originally published as a serial in the *St. Nicholas Magazine* between November 1885 and October 1886, then as a book by Scribner's in 1886. [The accompanying illustrations by Reginald Birch set fashion trends and *Little Lord Fauntleroy* also set a precedent in copyright law when in 1888 its author won a lawsuit against E. V. Seebohm over the rights to theatrical adaptations of the work.

Aa Bb Cc Dd Ee Ff Gg Hh Ii Jj Kk Ll Mm Nn Oo Pp Qq Rr Ss Tt Uu Vv Ww Xx Yy Zz

DejaVu Serif - 12

Little Lord Fauntleroy is the first children's novel written by English playwright and author Frances Hodgson Burnett. It was originally published as a serial in the *St. Nicholas Magazine* between November 1885 and October 1886, then as a book by Scribner's in 1886. [The accompanying illustrations by Reginald Birch set fashion trends and *Little Lord Fauntleroy* also set a precedent in copyright law when in 1888 its author won a lawsuit against E. V. Seebohm over the rights to theatrical adaptations of the work.

Aa Bb Cc Dd Ee Ff Gg Hh Ii Jj Kk Ll Mm Nn Oo Pp Qq Rr Ss Tt Uu Vv Ww Xx Yy Zz

DIRTYBAKERS DOZEN - 12

LITTLE LORD FAUNTLEROY IS THE FIRST CHILDREN'S NOVEL WRITTEN BY ENGLISH PLAYWRIGHT AND AUTHOR FRANCES HODGSON BURNETT. IT WAS ORIGINALLY PUBLISHED AS A SERIAL IN THE *ST. NICHOLAS MAGAZINE* BETWEEN NOVEMBER 1885 AND OCTOBER 1886, THEN AS A BOOK BY SCRIBNER'S IN 1886. ᴸTHE ACCOMPANYING ILLUSTRATIONS BY REGINALD BIRCH SET FASHION TRENDS AND *LITTLE LORD FAUNTLEROY* ALSO SET A PRECEDENT IN COPYRIGHT LAW WHEN IN 1888 ITS AUTHOR WON A LAWSUIT AGAINST E. V. SEEBOHM OVER THE RIGHTS TO THEATRICAL ADAPTATIONS OF THE WORK.

AA BB CC DD EE FF GG HH II JJ KK LL MM NN OO PP QQ RR SS TT UU VV WW XX YY ZZ

Ebrima - 12

Little Lord Fauntleroy is the first children's novel written by English playwright and author Frances Hodgson Burnett. It was originally published as a serial in the *St. Nicholas Magazine* between November 1885 and October 1886, then as a book by Scribner's in 1886. [1]The accompanying illustrations by Reginald Birch set fashion trends and *Little Lord Fauntleroy* also set a precedent in copyright law when in 1888 its author won a lawsuit against E. V. Seebohm over the rights to theatrical adaptations of the work.

Aa Bb Cc Dd Ee Ff Gg Hh Ii Jj Kk Ll Mm Nn Oo Pp Qq Rr Ss Tt Uu Vv Ww Xx Yy Zz

Elephant - 12

Little Lord Fauntleroy is the first children's novel written by English playwright and author Frances Hodgson Burnett. It was originally published as a serial in the *St. Nicholas Magazine* between November 1885 and October 1886, then as a book by Scribner's in 1886. The accompanying illustrations by Reginald Birch set fashion trends and *Little Lord Fauntleroy* also set a precedent in copyright law when in 1888 its author won a lawsuit against E. V. Seebohm over the rights to theatrical adaptations of the work.

Aa Bb Cc Dd Ee Ff Gg Hh Ii Jj Kk Ll Mm Nn Oo Pp Qq Rr Ss Tt Uu Vv Ww Xx Yy Zz

Eras Demi ITC - *12*

Little Lord Fauntleroy is the first children's novel written by English playwright and author Frances Hodgson Burnett. It was originally published as a serial in the *St. Nicholas Magazine* between November 1885 and October 1886, then as a book by Scribner's in 1886. [The accompanying illustrations by Reginald Birch set fashion trends and *Little Lord Fauntleroy* also set a precedent in copyright law when in 1888 its author won a lawsuit against E. V. Seebohm over the rights to theatrical adaptations of the work.

Aa Bb Cc Dd Ee Ff Gg Hh Ii Jj Kk Ll Mm Nn Oo Pp Qq Rr Ss Tt Uu Vv Ww Xx Yy Zz

Comparative Fonts

Estrangelo Edessa - 12

Little Lord Fauntleroy is the first children's novel written by English playwright and author Frances Hodgson Burnett. It was originally published as a serial in the *St. Nicholas Magazine* between November 1885 and October 1886, then as a book by Scribner's in 1886. [The accompanying illustrations by Reginald Birch set fashion trends and *Little Lord Fauntleroy* also set a precedent in copyright law when in 1888 its author won a lawsuit against E. V. Seebohm over the rights to theatrical adaptations of the work.

Aa Bb Cc Dd Ee Ff Gg Hh Ii Jj Kk Ll Mm Nn Oo Pp Qq Rr Ss Tt Uu Vv Ww Xx Yy Zz

Comparative Fonts

Euphemia   - 12

Little Lord Fauntleroy is the first children's novel written by English playwright and author Frances Hodgson Burnett. It was originally published as a serial in the *St. Nicholas Magazine* between November 1885 and October 1886, then as a book by Scribner's in 1886. ᶦThe accompanying illustrations by Reginald Birch set fashion trends and *Little Lord Fauntleroy* also set a precedent in copyright law when in 1888 its author won a lawsuit against E. V. Seebohm over the rights to theatrical adaptations of the work.

Aa Bb Cc Dd Ee Ff Gg Hh Ii Jj Kk Ll Mm Nn Oo Pp Qq Rr Ss Tt Uu Vv Ww Xx Yy Zz

Comparative Fonts

Franklin Gothic Book   - 12

Little Lord Fauntleroy is the first children's novel written by English playwright and author Frances Hodgson Burnett. It was originally published as a serial in the *St. Nicholas Magazine* between November 1885 and October 1886, then as a book by Scribner's in 1886. [The accompanying illustrations by Reginald Birch set fashion trends and *Little Lord Fauntleroy* also set a precedent in copyright law when in 1888 its author won a lawsuit against E. V. Seebohm over the rights to theatrical adaptations of the work.

Aa Bb Cc Dd Ee Ff Gg Hh Ii Jj Kk Ll Mm Nn Oo Pp Qq Rr Ss Tt Uu Vv Ww Xx Yy Zz

Franklin Gothic Demi   - 12

Little Lord Fauntleroy is the first children's novel
written by English playwright and author Frances
Hodgson Burnett. It was originally published as a
serial in the *St. Nicholas Magazine* between
November 1885 and October 1886, then as a book
by Scribner's in 1886. [The accompanying
illustrations by Reginald Birch set fashion trends
and *Little Lord Fauntleroy* also set a precedent in
copyright law when in 1888 its author won a lawsuit
against E. V. Seebohm over the rights to theatrical
adaptations of the work.

Aa Bb Cc Dd Ee Ff Gg Hh Ii Jj Kk Ll Mm Nn Oo Pp Qq
Rr Ss Tt Uu Vv Ww Xx Yy Zz

Franklin Gothic Heavy   - 12

Little Lord Fauntleroy is the first children's novel written by English playwright and author Frances Hodgson Burnett. It was originally published as a serial in the *St. Nicholas Magazine* between November 1885 and October 1886, then as a book by Scribner's in 1886. ᶦThe accompanying illustrations by Reginald Birch set fashion trends and *Little Lord Fauntleroy* also set a precedent in copyright law when in 1888 its author won a lawsuit against E. V. Seebohm over the rights to theatrical adaptations of the work.

Aa Bb Cc Dd Ee Ff Gg Hh Ii Jj Kk Ll Mm Nn Oo Pp Qq Rr Ss Tt Uu Vv Ww Xx Yy Zz

Comparative Fonts

Franklin Gothic Medium   - 12

Little Lord Fauntleroy is the first children's novel
written by English playwright and author Frances
Hodgson Burnett. It was originally published as a
serial in the *St. Nicholas Magazine* between
November 1885 and October 1886, then as a book
by Scribner's in 1886. ⸢The accompanying
illustrations by Reginald Birch set fashion trends and
Little Lord Fauntleroy also set a precedent in
copyright law when in 1888 its author won a lawsuit
against E. V. Seebohm over the rights to theatrical
adaptations of the work.

Aa Bb Cc Dd Ee Ff Gg Hh Ii Jj Kk Ll Mm Nn Oo Pp Qq
Rr Ss Tt Uu Vv Ww Xx Yy Zz

Comparative Fonts

Franklin Gothis Medium Condense   - 12

Little Lord Fauntleroy is the first children's novel written by
English playwright and author Frances Hodgson Burnett. It was
originally published as a serial in the *St. Nicholas Magazine*
between November 1885 and October 1886, then as a book by
Scribner's in 1886. The accompanying illustrations by
Reginald Birch set fashion trends and *Little Lord Fauntleroy*
also set a precedent in copyright law when in 1888 its author
won a lawsuit against E. V. Seebohm over the rights to
theatrical adaptations of the work.

Aa Bb Cc Dd Ee Ff Gg Hh Ii Jj Kk Ll Mm Nn Oo Pp Qq Rr Ss Tt Uu
Vv Ww Xx Yy Zz

Gentium Basic   - 12

Little Lord Fauntleroy is the first children's novel written by English playwright and author Frances Hodgson Burnett. It was originally published as a serial in the *St. Nicholas Magazine* between November 1885 and October 1886, then as a book by Scribner's in 1886. [The accompanying illustrations by Reginald Birch set fashion trends and *Little Lord Fauntleroy* also set a precedent in copyright law when in 1888 its author won a lawsuit against E. V. Seebohm over the rights to theatrical adaptations of the work.

Aa Bb Cc Dd Ee Ff Gg Hh Ii Jj Kk Ll Mm Nn Oo Pp Qq Rr Ss Tt Uu Vv Ww Xx Yy Zz

Gentium Book Basic - 12

Little Lord Fauntleroy is the first children's novel
written by English playwright and author Frances
Hodgson Burnett. It was originally published as a
serial in the *St. Nicholas Magazine* between November
1885 and October 1886, then as a book by Scribner's in
1886. ⌈The accompanying illustrations by Reginald
Birch set fashion trends and *Little Lord Fauntleroy* also
set a precedent in copyright law when in 1888 its
author won a lawsuit against E. V. Seebohm over the
rights to theatrical adaptations of the work.

Aa Bb Cc Dd Ee Ff Gg Hh Ii Jj Kk Ll Mm Nn Oo Pp Qq Rr
Ss Tt Uu Vv Ww Xx Yy Zz

Georgia   - 12

Little Lord Fauntleroy is the first children's novel written by English playwright and author Frances Hodgson Burnett. It was originally published as a serial in the *St. Nicholas Magazine* between November 1885 and October 1886, then as a book by Scribner's in 1886. ⌐The accompanying illustrations by Reginald Birch set fashion trends and *Little Lord Fauntleroy* also set a precedent in copyright law when in 1888 its author won a lawsuit against E. V. Seebohm over the rights to theatrical adaptations of the work.

Aa Bb Cc Dd Ee Ff Gg Hh Ii Jj Kk Ll Mm Nn Oo Pp Qq Rr Ss Tt Uu Vv Ww Xx Yy Zz

Gisha - 12

Little Lord Fauntleroy is the first children's novel written by English playwright and author Frances Hodgson Burnett. It was originally published as a serial in the *St. Nicholas Magazine* between November 1885 and October 1886, then as a book by Scribner's in 1886. [The accompanying illustrations by Reginald Birch set fashion trends and *Little Lord Fauntleroy* also set a precedent in copyright law when in 1888 its author won a lawsuit against E. V. Seebohm over the rights to theatrical adaptations of the work.

Aa Bb Cc Dd Ee Ff Gg Hh Ii Jj Kk Ll Mm Nn Oo Pp Qq Rr Ss Tt Uu Vv Ww Xx Yy Zz

Comparative Fonts

Gulim – 12

Little Lord Fauntleroy is the first children's novel written by English playwright and author Frances Hodgson Burnett. It was originally published as a serial in the *St. Nicholas Magazine* between November 1885 and October 1886, then as a book by Scribner's in 1886. [1]The accompanying illustrations by Reginald Birch set fashion trends and *Little Lord Fauntleroy* also set a precedent in copyright law when in 1888 its author won a lawsuit against E. V. Seebohm over the rights to theatrical adaptations of the work.

Aa Bb Cc Dd Ee Ff Gg Hh Ii Jj Kk Ll Mm Nn Oo Pp Qq Rr Ss Tt Uu Vv Ww Xx Yy Zz

Comparative Fonts

GungsuhChe - 12

Little Lord Fauntleroy is the first children's novel written by English playwright and author Frances Hodgson Burnett. It was originally published as a serial in the *St. Nicholas Magazine* between November 1885 and October 1886, then as a book by Scribner's in 1886. [The accompanying illustrations by Reginald Birch set fashion trends and *Little Lord Fauntleroy* also set a precedent in copyright law when in 1888 its author won a lawsuit against E. V. Seebohm over the rights to theatrical adaptations of the work.

Aa Bb Cc Dd Ee Ff Gg Hh Ii Jj Kk Ll Mm Nn Oo
Pp Qq Rr Ss Tt Uu Vv Ww Xx Yy Zz

Comparative Fonts

Harlow Solid Italic 12

Little Lord Fauntleroy is the first children's novel written by English playwright and author Frances Hodgson Burnett. It was originally published as a serial in the St. Nicholas Magazine between November 1885 and October 1886, then as a book by Scribner's in 1886. The accompanying illustrations by Reginald Birch set fashion trends and Little Lord Fauntleroy also set a precedent in copyright law when in 1888 its author won a lawsuit against E. V. Seebohm over the rights to theatrical adaptations of the work.

Aa Bb Cc Dd Ee Ff Gg Hh Ii Jj Kk Ll Mm Nn Oo Pp Qq Rr Ss Tt Uu Vv Ww Xx Yy Zz

Comparative Fonts

Highway to Heck · 12

Little Lord Fauntleroy is the first children's novel written by English playwright and author Frances Hodgson Burnett. It was originally published as a serial in the *St. Nicholas Magazine* between November 1885 and October 1886, then as a book by Scribner's in 1886. [The accompanying illustrations by Reginald Birch set fashion trends and *Little Lord Fauntleroy* also set a precedent in copyright law when in 1888 its author won a lawsuit against E. V. Seebohm over the rights to theatrical adaptations of the work.

Aa Bb Cc Dd Ee Ff Gg Hh Ii Jj Kk Ll Mm Nn Oo Pp Qq Rr Ss Tt Uu Vv Ww Xx Yy Zz

Comparative Fonts

Imprint MT Shadow - 12

Little Lord Fauntleroy is the first children's novel written by English playwright and author Frances Hodgson Burnett. It was originally published as a serial in the *St. Nicholas Magazine* between November 1885 and October 1886, then as a book by Scribner's in 1886. [The accompanying illustrations by Reginald Birch set fashion trends and *Little Lord Fauntleroy* also set a precedent in copyright law when in 1888 its author won a lawsuit against E. V. Seebohm over the rights to theatrical adaptations of the work.

Aa Bb Cc Dd Ee Ff Gg Hh Ii Jj Kk Ll Mm Nn Oo Pp Qq Rr Ss Tt Uu Vv Ww Xx Yy Zz

Comparative Fonts

Iskoola Pota   - 12

Little Lord Fauntleroy is the first children's novel
written by English playwright and author Frances
Hodgson Burnett. It was originally published as a serial
in the *St. Nicholas Magazine* between November 1885
and October 1886, then as a book by Scribner's in 1886.
The accompanying illustrations by Reginald Birch set
fashion trends and *Little Lord Fauntleroy* also set a
precedent in copyright law when in 1888 its author won
a lawsuit against E. V. Seebohm over the rights to
theatrical adaptations of the work.

Aa Bb Cc Dd Ee Ff Gg Hh Ii Jj Kk Ll Mm Nn Oo Pp Qq
Rr Ss Tt Uu Vv Ww Xx Yy Zz

Jokerman - 12

Little Lord Fauntleroy is the first children's novel written by English playwright and author Frances Hodgson Burnett. It was originally published as a serial in the *St. Nicholas Magazine* between November 1885 and October 1886, then as a book by Scribner's in 1886. The accompanying illustrations by Reginald Birch set fashion trends and *Little Lord Fauntleroy* also set a precedent in copyright law when in 1888 its author won a lawsuit against E. V. Seebohm over the rights to theatrical adaptations of the work.

Aa Bb Cc Dd Ee Ff Gg Hh Ii Jj Kk Ll Mm Nn Oo Pp Qq Rr Ss Tt Uu Vv Ww Xx Yy Zz

Comparative Fonts

Khmer UI   - 12

Little Lord Fauntleroy is the first children's novel written by English playwright and author Frances Hodgson Burnett. It was originally published as a serial in the *St. Nicholas Magazine* between November 1885 and October 1886, then as a book by Scribner's in 1886. [The accompanying illustrations by Reginald Birch set fashion trends and *Little Lord Fauntleroy* also set a precedent in copyright law when in 1888 its author won a lawsuit against E. V. Seebohm over the rights to theatrical adaptations of the work.

Aa Bb Cc Dd Ee Ff Gg Hh Ii Jj Kk Ll Mm Nn Oo Pp Qq Rr Ss Tt Uu Vv Ww Xx Yy Zz

Kristen ITC - 12

Little Lord Fauntleroy is the first children's novel written by English playwright and author Frances Hodgson Burnett. It was originally published as a serial in the *St. Nicholas Magazine* between November 1885 and October 1886, then as a book by Scribner's in 1886. The accompanying illustrations by Reginald Birch set fashion trends and *Little Lord Fauntleroy* also set a precedent in copyright law when in 1888 its author won a lawsuit against E. V. Seebohm over the rights to theatrical adaptations of the work.

Aa Bb Cc Dd Ee Ff Gg Hh Ii Jj Kk Ll Mm Nn Oo Pp Qq Rr Ss Tt Uu Vv Ww Xx Yy Zz

Comparative Fonts

Lao UI - 12

Little Lord Fauntleroy is the first children's novel written by English playwright and author Frances Hodgson Burnett. It was originally published as a serial in the *St. Nicholas Magazine* between November 1885 and October 1886, then as a book by Scribner's in 1886. [The accompanying illustrations by Reginald Birch set fashion trends and *Little Lord Fauntleroy* also set a precedent in copyright law when in 1888 its author won a lawsuit against E. V. Seebohm over the rights to theatrical adaptations of the work.

Aa Bb Cc Dd Ee Ff Gg Hh Ii Jj Kk Ll Mm Nn Oo Pp Qq Rr Ss Tt Uu Vv Ww Xx Yy Zz

Leelawadee   - 12

Little Lord Fauntleroy is the first children's novel written by English playwright and author Frances Hodgson Burnett. It was originally published as a serial in the *St. Nicholas Magazine* between November 1885 and October 1886, then as a book by Scribner's in 1886. [1]The accompanying illustrations by Reginald Birch set fashion trends and *Little Lord Fauntleroy* also set a precedent in copyright law when in 1888 its author won a lawsuit against E. V. Seebohm over the rights to theatrical adaptations of the work.

Aa Bb Cc Dd Ee Ff Gg Hh Ii Jj Kk Ll Mm Nn Oo Pp Qq Rr Ss Tt Uu Vv Ww Xx Yy Zz

Comparative Fonts

Lucida Bright – 12

Little Lord Fauntleroy is the first children's novel written by English playwright and author Frances Hodgson Burnett. It was originally published as a serial in the *St. Nicholas Magazine* between November 1885 and October 1886, then as a book by Scribner's in 1886. ᴵThe accompanying illustrations by Reginald Birch set fashion trends and *Little Lord Fauntleroy* also set a precedent in copyright law when in 1888 its author won a lawsuit against E. V. Seebohm over the rights to theatrical adaptations of the work.

Aa Bb Cc Dd Ee Ff Gg Hh Ii Jj Kk Ll Mm Nn Oo Pp Qq Rr Ss Tt Uu Vv Ww Xx Yy Zz

Luida Calligraphy   - 12

Little Lord Fauntleroy is the first children's novel written by English playwright and author Frances Hodgson Burnett. It was originally published as a serial in the *St. Nicholas Magazine* between November 1885 and October 1886, then as a book by Scribner's in 1886. [The accompanying illustrations by Reginald Birch set fashion trends and *Little Lord Fauntleroy* also set a precedent in copyright law when in 1888 its author won a lawsuit against E. V. Seebohm over the rights to theatrical adaptations of the work.

Aa Bb Cc Dd Ee Ff Gg Hh Ii Jj Kk Ll Mm Nn Oo Pp Qq Rr Ss Tt Uu Vv Ww Xx Yy Zz

Comparative Fonts

Lucida Console   - 12

Little Lord Fauntleroy is the first children's novel written by English playwright and author Frances Hodgson Burnett. It was originally published as a serial in the *St. Nicholas Magazine* between November 1885 and October 1886, then as a book by Scribner's in 1886. ⌐The accompanying illustrations by Reginald Birch set fashion trends and *Little Lord Fauntleroy* also set a precedent in copyright law when in 1888 its author won a lawsuit against E. V. Seebohm over the rights to theatrical adaptations of the work.

Aa Bb Cc Dd Ee Ff Gg Hh Ii Jj Kk Ll Mm
Nn Oo Pp Qq Rr Ss Tt Uu Vv Ww Xx Yy Zz

Lucida Fax - 12

Little Lord Fauntleroy is the first children's novel written by English playwright and author Frances Hodgson Burnett. It was originally published as a serial in the *St. Nicholas Magazine* between November 1885 and October 1886, then as a book by Scribner's in 1886. ᴵThe accompanying illustrations by Reginald Birch set fashion trends and *Little Lord Fauntleroy* also set a precedent in copyright law when in 1888 its author won a lawsuit against E. V. Seebohm over the rights to theatrical adaptations of the work.

Aa Bb Cc Dd Ee Ff Gg Hh Ii Jj Kk Ll Mm Nn Oo Pp Qq Rr Ss Tt Uu Vv Ww Xx Yy Zz

Comparative Fonts

Lucida Handwriting - 12

Little Lord Fauntleroy is the first children's novel written by English playwright and author Frances Hodgson Burnett. It was originally published as a serial in the St. Nicholas Magazine between November 1885 and October 1886, then as a book by Scribner's in 1886. [1]The accompanying illustrations by Reginald Birch set fashion trends and *Little Lord Fauntleroy* also set a precedent in copyright law when in 1888 its author won a lawsuit against E. V. Seebohm over the rights to theatrical adaptations of the work.

Aa Bb Cc Dd Ee Ff Gg Hh Ii Jj Kk Ll Mm Nn Oo Pp Qq Rr Ss Tt Uu Vv Ww Xx Yy Zz

Lucida Sans Typewriter   - 12

Little Lord Fauntleroy is the first children's novel written by English playwright and author Frances Hodgson Burnett. It was originally published as a serial in the *St. Nicholas Magazine* between November 1885 and October 1886, then as a book by Scribner's in 1886. ꞌThe accompanying illustrations by Reginald Birch set fashion trends and *Little Lord Fauntleroy* also set a precedent in copyright law when in 1888 its author won a lawsuit against E. V. Seebohm over the rights to theatrical adaptations of the work.

Aa Bb Cc Dd Ee Ff Gg Hh Ii Jj Kk Ll Mm Nn Oo Pp Qq Rr Ss Tt Uu Vv Ww Xx Yy Zz

Comparative Fonts

Maiandra GD - 12

Little Lord Fauntleroy is the first children's novel
written by English playwright and author Frances
Hodgson Burnett. It was originally published as a
serial in the *St. Nicholas Magazine* between
November 1885 and October 1886, then as a book
by Scribner's in 1886. The accompanying
illustrations by Reginald Birch set fashion trends and
Little Lord Fauntleroy also set a precedent in
copyright law when in 1888 its author won a
lawsuit against E. V. Seebohm over the rights to
theatrical adaptations of the work.

Aa Bb Cc Dd Ee Ff Gg Hh Ii Jj Kk Ll Mm Nn Oo Pp
Qq Rr Ss Tt Uu Vv Ww Xx Yy Zz

MAIL RAY STUFF - 12

LITTLE LORD FAUNTLEROY IS THE FIRST CHILDREN'S NOVEL WRITTEN BY ENGLISH PLAYWRIGHT AND AUTHOR FRANCES HODGSON BURNETT. IT WAS ORIGINALLY PUBLISHED AS A SERIAL IN THE ST. NICHOLAS MAGAZINE BETWEEN NOVEMBER 1885 AND OCTOBER 1886, THEN AS A BOOK BY SCRIBNER'S IN 1886. [1]THE ACCOMPANYING ILLUSTRATIONS BY REGINALD BIRCH SET FASHION TRENDS AND LITTLE LORD FAUNTLEROY ALSO SET A PRECEDENT IN COPYRIGHT LAW WHEN IN 1888 ITS AUTHOR WON A LAWSUIT AGAINST E. V. SEEBOHM OVER THE RIGHTS TO THEATRICAL ADAPTATIONS OF THE WORK.

AA BB CC DD EE FF GG HH II JJ KK LL MM NN OO PP QQ RR SS TT UU VV WW XX YY ZZ

Microsoft New Tai Lue - 12

Little Lord Fauntleroy is the first children's novel written by English playwright and author Frances Hodgson Burnett. It was originally published as a serial in the *St. Nicholas Magazine* between November 1885 and October 1886, then as a book by Scribner's in 1886. [The accompanying illustrations by Reginald Birch set fashion trends and *Little Lord Fauntleroy* also set a precedent in copyright law when in 1888 its author won a lawsuit against E. V. Seebohm over the rights to theatrical adaptations of the work.

Aa Bb Cc Dd Ee Ff Gg Hh Ii Jj Kk Ll Mm Nn Oo Pp Qq Rr Ss Tt Uu Vv Ww Xx Yy Zz

Micrsoft Sans Seriff - 12

Little Lord Fauntleroy is the first children's novel written by English playwright and author Frances Hodgson Burnett. It was originally published as a serial in the *St. Nicholas Magazine* between November 1885 and October 1886, then as a book by Scribner's in 1886. [The accompanying illustrations by Reginald Birch set fashion trends and *Little Lord Fauntleroy* also set a precedent in copyright law when in 1888 its author won a lawsuit against E. V. Seebohm over the rights to theatrical adaptations of the work.

Aa Bb Cc Dd Ee Ff Gg Hh Ii Jj Kk Ll Mm Nn Oo Pp Qq Rr Ss Tt Uu Vv Ww Xx Yy Zz

Comparative Fonts

NightpOrber ~ 12

Little Lord Fauntleroy is the first children's novel written by English playwright and author Frances Hodgson Burnett. It was originally published as a serial in the *St. Nicholas Magazine* between November 1885 and October 1886, then as a book by Scribner's in 1886. [The accompanying illustrations by Reginald Birch set fashion trends and *Little Lord Fauntleroy* also set a precedent in copyright law when in 1888 its author won a lawsuit against E. V. Seebohm over the rights to theatrical adaptations of the work.

Aa Bb Cc Dd Ee Ff Gg Hh Ii Jj Kk Ll Mm Nn Oo Pp Qq Rr Ss Tt Uu Vv Ww Xx Yy Zz

Comparative Fonts

NSimSun – 12

Little Lord Fauntleroy is the first children's novel written by English playwright and author Frances Hodgson Burnett. It was originally published as a serial in the *St. Nicholas Magazine* between November 1885 and October 1886, then as a book by Scribner's in 1886. [The accompanying illustrations by Reginald Birch set fashion trends and *Little Lord Fauntleroy* also set a precedent in copyright law when in 1888 its author won a lawsuit against E. V. Seebohm over the rights to theatrical adaptations of the work.

Aa Bb Cc Dd Ee Ff Gg Hh Ii Jj Kk Ll Mm Nn Oo Pp Qq Rr Ss Tt Uu Vv Ww Xx Yy Zz

Comparative Fonts

Nyala - 12

Little Lord Fauntleroy is the first children's novel written by English playwright and author Frances Hodgson Burnett. It was originally published as a serial in the *St. Nicholas Magazine* between November 1885 and October 1886, then as a book by Scribner's in 1886. [The accompanying illustrations by Reginald Birch set fashion trends and *Little Lord Fauntleroy* also set a precedent in copyright law when in 1888 its author won a lawsuit against E. V. Seebohm over the rights to theatrical adaptations of the work.

Aa Bb Cc Dd Ee Ff Gg Hh Ii Jj Kk Ll Mm Nn Oo Pp Qq Rr Ss Tt Uu Vv Ww Xx Yy Zz

Old English Text   - 12

Little Lord Fauntleroy is the first children's novel written by English playwright and author Frances Hodgson Burnett. It was originally published as a serial in the St. Nicholas Magazine between November 1885 and October 1886, then as a book by Scribner's in 1886. The accompanying illustrations by Reginald Birch set fashion trends and *Little Lord Fauntleroy* also set a precedent in copyright law when in 1888 its author won a lawsuit against E. V. Seebohm over the rights to theatrical adaptations of the work.

Aa Bb Cc Dd Ee Ff Gg Hh Ii Jj Kk Ll Mm Nn Oo Pp Qq Rr Ss Tt Uu Vv Ww Xx Yy Zz

Comparative Fonts

Palatino Linotype   - 12

Little Lord Fauntleroy is the first children's novel written by English playwright and author Frances Hodgson Burnett. It was originally published as a serial in the *St. Nicholas Magazine* between November 1885 and October 1886, then as a book by Scribner's in 1886. ⌐The accompanying illustrations by Reginald Birch set fashion trends and *Little Lord Fauntleroy* also set a precedent in copyright law when in 1888 its author won a lawsuit against E. V. Seebohm over the rights to theatrical adaptations of the work.

Aa Bb Cc Dd Ee Ff Gg Hh Ii Jj Kk Ll Mm Nn Oo Pp Qq Rr Ss Tt Uu Vv Ww Xx Yy Zz

Comparative Fonts

Papyrus ~ 12

Little Lord Fauntleroy is the first children's novel written by English playwright and author Frances Hodgson Burnett. It was originally published as a serial in the *St. Nicholas Magazine* between November 1885 and October 1886, then as a book by Scribner's in 1886. The accompanying illustrations by Reginald Birch set fashion trends and *Little Lord Fauntleroy* also set a precedent in copyright law when in 1888 its author won a lawsuit against E. V. Seebohm over the rights to theatrical adaptations of the work.

Aa Bb Cc Dd Ee Ff Gg Hh Ii Jj Kk Ll Mm Nn Oo Pp Qq Rr Ss Tt Uu Vv Ww Xx Yy Zz

Comparative Fonts

Perpetua- 12

Little Lord Fauntleroy is the first children's novel written by
English playwright and author Frances Hodgson Burnett. It was
originally published as a serial in the *St. Nicholas Magazine*
between November 1885 and October 1886, then as a book by
Scribner's in 1886. [1]The accompanying illustrations by Reginald
Birch set fashion trends and *Little Lord Fauntleroy* also set a
precedent in copyright law when in 1888 its author won a
lawsuit against E. V. Seebohm over the rights to theatrical
adaptations of the work.

Aa Bb Cc Dd Ee Ff Gg Hh Ii Jj Kk Ll Mm Nn Oo Pp Qq Rr Ss
Tt Uu Vv Ww Xx Yy Zz

Plasntagenet Cherokee - 12

Little Lord Fauntleroy is the first children's novel written by English playwright and author Frances Hodgson Burnett. It was originally published as a serial in the *St. Nicholas Magazine* between November 1885 and October 1886, then as a book by Scribner's in 1886. [The accompanying illustrations by Reginald Birch set fashion trends and *Little Lord Fauntleroy* also set a precedent in copyright law when in 1888 its author won a lawsuit against E. V. Seebohm over the rights to theatrical adaptations of the work.

Aa Bb Cc Dd Ee Ff Gg Hh Ii Jj Kk Ll Mm Nn Oo Pp Qq Rr Ss Tt Uu Vv Ww Xx Yy Zz

Comparative Fonts

Playbill - 12

Little Lord Fauntleroy is the first children's novel written by English playwright and author Frances Hodgson Burnett. It was originally published as a serial in the *St. Nicholas Magazine* between November 1885 and October 1886, then as a book by Scribner's in 1886. The accompanying illustrations by Reginald Birch set fashion trends and *Little Lord Fauntleroy* also set a precedent in copyright law when in 1888 its author won a lawsuit against E. V. Seebohm over the rights to theatrical adaptations of the work.

Aa Bb Cc Dd Ee Ff Gg Hh Ii Jj Kk Ll Mm Nn Oo Pp Qq Rr Ss Tt Uu Vv Ww Xx Yy Zz

Comparative Fonts

Poor Richard ~ 12

Little Lord Fauntleroy is the first children's novel written by English playwright and author Frances Hodgson Burnett. It was originally published as a serial in the *St. Nicholas Magazine* between November 1885 and October 1886, then as a book by Scribner's in 1886. The accompanying illustrations by Reginald Birch set fashion trends and *Little Lord Fauntleroy* also set a precedent in copyright law when in 1888 its author won a lawsuit against E. V. Seebohm over the rights to theatrical adaptations of the work.

Aa Bb Cc Dd Ee Ff Gg Hh Ii Jj Kk Ll Mm Nn Oo Pp Qq Rr Ss Tt Uu Vv Ww Xx Yy Zz

PRIME MINISTER OF CANADA – 12

LITTLE LORD FAUNTLEROY IS THE FIRST CHILDREN'S NOVEL WRITTEN BY ENGLISH PLAYWRIGHT AND AUTHOR FRANCES HODGSON BURNETT. IT WAS ORIGINALLY PUBLISHED AS A SERIAL IN THE *ST. NICHOLAS MAGAZINE* BETWEEN NOVEMBER 1885 AND OCTOBER 1886, THEN AS A BOOK BY SCRIBNER'S IN 1886. [THE ACCOMPANYING ILLUSTRATIONS BY REGINALD BIRCH SET FASHION TRENDS AND *LITTLE LORD FAUNTLEROY* ALSO SET A PRECEDENT IN COPYRIGHT LAW WHEN IN 1888 ITS AUTHOR WON A LAWSUIT AGAINST E. V. SEEBOHM OVER THE RIGHTS TO THEATRICAL ADAPTATIONS OF THE WORK.

AA BB CC DD EE FF GG HH II JJ KK LL MM NN OO PP QQ RR SS TT UU VV WW XX YY ZZ

RADIO STARS - 12

LITTLE LORD FAUNTLEROY IS THE FIRST CHILDREN'S NOVEL WRITTEN BY ENGLISH PLAYWRIGHT AND AUTHOR FRANCES HODGSON BURNETT. IT WAS ORIGINALLY PUBLISHED AS A SERIAL IN THE *ST. NICHOLAS MAGAZINE* BETWEEN NOVEMBER 1885 AND OCTOBER 1886, THEN AS A BOOK BY SCRIBNER'S IN 1886. THE ACCOMPANYING ILLUSTRATIONS BY REGINALD BIRCH SET FASHION TRENDS AND *LITTLE LORD FAUNTLEROY* ALSO SET A PRECEDENT IN COPYRIGHT LAW WHEN IN 1888 ITS AUTHOR WON A LAWSUIT AGAINST E. V. SEEBOHM OVER THE RIGHTS TO THEATRICAL ADAPTATIONS OF THE WORK.

AA BB CC DD EE FF GG HH II JJ KK LL MM NN OO PP QQ RR SS TT UU VV WW XX YY ZZ

Ravie - 12

Little Lord Fauntleroy is the first children's novel written by English playwright and author Frances Hodgson Burnett. It was originally published as a serial in the *St. Nicholas Magazine* between November 1885 and October 1886, then as a book by Scribner's in 1886. The accompanying illustrations by Reginald Birch set fashion trends and *Little Lord Fauntleroy* also set a precedent in copyright law when in 1888 its author won a lawsuit against E. V. Seebohm over the rights to theatrical adaptations of the work.

Aa Bb Cc Dd Ee Ff Gg Hh Ii Jj Kk Ll Mm Nn Oo Pp Qq Rr Ss Tt Uu Vv Ww Xx Yy Zz

Rockwell - 12

Little Lord Fauntleroy is the first children's novel written by English playwright and author Frances Hodgson Burnett. It was originally published as a serial in the *St. Nicholas Magazine* between November 1885 and October 1886, then as a book by Scribner's in 1886. [The accompanying illustrations by Reginald Birch set fashion trends and *Little Lord Fauntleroy* also set a precedent in copyright law when in 1888 its author won a lawsuit against E. V. Seebohm over the rights to theatrical adaptations of the work.

Aa Bb Cc Dd Ee Ff Gg Hh Ii Jj Kk Ll Mm Nn Oo Pp Qq Rr Ss Tt Uu Vv Ww Xx Yy Zz

Rockwell Condensed - 12

Little Lord Fauntleroy is the first children's novel written by English playwright and author Frances Hodgson Burnett. It was originally published as a serial in the *St. Nicholas Magazine* between November 1885 and October 1886, then as a book by Scribner's in 1886. The accompanying illustrations by Reginald Birch set fashion trends and *Little Lord Fauntleroy* also set a precedent in copyright law when in 1888 its author won a lawsuit against E. V. Seebohm over the rights to theatrical adaptations of the work.

Aa Bb Cc Dd Ee Ff Gg Hh Ii Jj Kk Ll Mm Nn Oo Pp Qq Rr Ss Tt Uu Vv Ww Xx Yy Zz

Script MT Bold - 12

Little Lord Fauntleroy is the first children's novel written by English playwright and author Frances Hodgson Burnett. It was originally published as a serial in the St. Nicholas Magazine between November 1885 and October 1886, then as a book by Scribner's in 1886. [The accompanying illustrations by Reginald Birch set fashion trends and Little Lord Fauntleroy also set a precedent in copyright law when in 1888 its author won a lawsuit against E. V. Seebohm over the rights to theatrical adaptations of the work.

Aa Bb Cc Dd Ee Ff Gg Hh Ii Jj Kk Ll Mm Nn Oo Pp Qq Rr Ss Tt Uu Vv Ww Xx Yy Zz

Comparative Fonts

Segoe Print – 12

Little Lord Fauntleroy is the first children's novel written by English playwright and author Frances Hodgson Burnett. It was originally published as a serial in the *St. Nicholas Magazine* between November 1885 and October 1886, then as a book by Scribner's in 1886. [The accompanying illustrations by Reginald Birch set fashion trends and *Little Lord Fauntleroy* also set a precedent in copyright law when in 1888 its author won a lawsuit against E. V. Seebohm over the rights to theatrical adaptations of the work.

Aa Bb Cc Dd Ee Ff Gg Hh Ii Jj Kk Ll Mm Nn Oo Pp Qq Rr Ss Tt Uu Vv Ww Xx Yy Zz

Comparative Fonts

Segoe UI - 12

Little Lord Fauntleroy is the first children's novel written by English playwright and author Frances Hodgson Burnett. It was originally published as a serial in the *St. Nicholas Magazine* between November 1885 and October 1886, then as a book by Scribner's in 1886. [The accompanying illustrations by Reginald Birch set fashion trends and *Little Lord Fauntleroy* also set a precedent in copyright law when in 1888 its author won a lawsuit against E. V. Seebohm over the rights to theatrical adaptations of the work.

Aa Bb Cc Dd Ee Ff Gg Hh Ii Jj Kk Ll Mm Nn Oo Pp Qq Rr Ss Tt Uu Vv Ww Xx Yy Zz

Segoe UI Semibold- 12

Little Lord Fauntleroy is the first children's novel written by English playwright and author Frances Hodgson Burnett. It was originally published as a serial in the *St. Nicholas Magazine* between November 1885 and October 1886, then as a book by Scribner's in 1886. [The accompanying illustrations by Reginald Birch set fashion trends and *Little Lord Fauntleroy* also set a precedent in copyright law when in 1888 its author won a lawsuit against E. V. Seebohm over the rights to theatrical adaptations of the work.

Aa Bb Cc Dd Ee Ff Gg Hh Ii Jj Kk Ll Mm Nn Oo Pp Qq Rr Ss Tt Uu Vv Ww Xx Yy Zz

SHLOP- 12

LITTLE LORD FAUNTLEROY IS THE FIRST CHILDREN'S NOVEL WRITTEN BY ENGLISH PLAYWRIGHT AND AUTHOR FRANCES HODGSON BURNETT. IT WAS ORIGINALLY PUBLISHED AS A SERIAL IN THE *ST. NICHOLAS MAGAZINE* BETWEEN NOVEMBER 1885 AND OCTOBER 1886, THEN AS A BOOK BY SCRIBNER'S IN 1886. ᶠTHE ACCOMPANYING ILLUSTRATIONS BY REGINALD BIRCH SET FASHION TRENDS AND *LITTLE LORD FAUNTLEROY* ALSO SET A PRECEDENT IN COPYRIGHT LAW WHEN IN 1888 ITS AUTHOR WON A LAWSUIT AGAINST E. V. SEEBOHM OVER THE RIGHTS TO THEATRICAL ADAPTATIONS OF THE WORK.

AA BB CC DD EE FF GG HH II JJ KK LL MM NN OO PP QQ RR SS TT UU VV WW XX YY ZZ

SHOWCARD GOTHIC- 12

LITTLE LORD FAUNTLEROY IS THE FIRST CHILDREN'S NOVEL WRITTEN BY ENGLISH PLAYWRIGHT AND AUTHOR FRANCES HODGSON BURNETT. IT WAS ORIGINALLY PUBLISHED AS A SERIAL IN THE *ST. NICHOLAS MAGAZINE* BETWEEN NOVEMBER 1885 AND OCTOBER 1886, THEN AS A BOOK BY SCRIBNER'S IN 1886. [THE ACCOMPANYING ILLUSTRATIONS BY REGINALD BIRCH SET FASHION TRENDS AND *LITTLE LORD FAUNTLEROY* ALSO SET A PRECEDENT IN COPYRIGHT LAW WHEN IN 1888 ITS AUTHOR WON A LAWSUIT AGAINST E. V. SEEBOHM OVER THE RIGHTS TO THEATRICAL ADAPTATIONS OF THE WORK.

AA BB CC DD EE FF GG HH II JJ KK LL MM NN OO PP QQ RR SS TT UU VV WW XX YY ZZ

Simplifid Arabic Fixed- 12

Little Lord Fauntleroy is the first children's novel written by English playwright and author Frances Hodgson Burnett. It was originally published as a serial in the *St. Nicholas Magazine* between November 1885 and October 1886, then as a book by Scribner's in 1886. [1]The accompanying illustrations by Reginald Birch set fashion trends and *Little Lord Fauntleroy* also set a precedent in copyright law when in 1888 its author won a lawsuit against E. V. Seebohm over the rights to theatrical adaptations of the work.

Aa Bb Cc Dd Ee Ff Gg Hh Ii Jj Kk Ll Mm
Nn Oo Pp Qq Rr Ss Tt Uu Vv Ww Xx Yy Zz

Comparative Fonts

Simsun 12

Little Lord Fauntleroy is the first children's novel written by English playwright and author Frances Hodgson Burnett. It was originally published as a serial in the *St. Nicholas Magazine* between November 1885 and October 1886, then as a book by Scribner's in 1886. The accompanying illustrations by Reginald Birch set fashion trends and *Little Lord Fauntleroy* also set a precedent in copyright law when in 1888 its author won a lawsuit against E. V. Seebohm over the rights to theatrical adaptations of the work.

Aa Bb Cc Dd Ee Ff Gg Hh Ii Jj Kk Ll Mm Nn Oo Pp Qq Rr Ss Tt Uu Vv Ww Xx Yy Zz

Snap ITC 12

Little Lord Fauntleroy is the first children's novel written by English playwright and author Frances Hodgson Burnett. It was originally published as a serial in the *St. Nicholas Magazine* between November 1885 and October 1886, then as a book by Scribner's in 1886. The accompanying illustrations by Reginald Birch set fashion trends and *Little Lord Fauntleroy* also set a precedent in copyright law when in 1888 its author won a lawsuit against E. V. Seebohm over the rights to theatrical adaptations of the work.

Aa Bb Cc Dd Ee Ff Gg Hh Ii Jj Kk Ll Mm Nn Oo Pp Qq Rr Ss Tt Uu Vv Ww Xx Yy Zz

STENCIL- 12

LITTLE LORD FAUNTLEROY IS THE FIRST CHILDREN'S NOVEL WRITTEN BY ENGLISH PLAYWRIGHT AND AUTHOR FRANCES HODGSON BURNETT. IT WAS ORIGINALLY PUBLISHED AS A SERIAL IN THE *ST. NICHOLAS MAGAZINE* BETWEEN NOVEMBER 1885 AND OCTOBER 1886, THEN AS A BOOK BY SCRIBNER'S IN 1886. THE ACCOMPANYING ILLUSTRATIONS BY REGINALD BIRCH SET FASHION TRENDS AND *LITTLE LORD FAUNTLEROY* ALSO SET A PRECEDENT IN COPYRIGHT LAW WHEN IN 1888 ITS AUTHOR WON A LAWSUIT AGAINST E. V. SEEBOHM OVER THE RIGHTS TO THEATRICAL ADAPTATIONS OF THE WORK.

AA BB CC DD EE FF GG HH II JJ KK LL MM NN OO PP QQ RR SS TT UU VV WW XX YY ZZ

Comparative Fonts

Sylfaen 12

Little Lord Fauntleroy is the first children's novel written by English playwright and author Frances Hodgson Burnett. It was originally published as a serial in the *St. Nicholas Magazine* between November 1885 and October 1886, then as a book by Scribner's in 1886. The accompanying illustrations by Reginald Birch set fashion trends and *Little Lord Fauntleroy* also set a precedent in copyright law when in 1888 its author won a lawsuit against E. V. Seebohm over the rights to theatrical adaptations of the work.

Aa Bb Cc Dd Ee Ff Gg Hh Ii Jj Kk Ll Mm Nn Oo Pp Qq Rr Ss Tt Uu Vv Ww Xx Yy Zz

Comparative Fonts

Tahoma 12

Little Lord Fauntleroy is the first children's novel written by English playwright and author Frances Hodgson Burnett. It was originally published as a serial in the *St. Nicholas Magazine* between November 1885 and October 1886, then as a book by Scribner's in 1886. ⌐The accompanying illustrations by Reginald Birch set fashion trends and *Little Lord Fauntleroy* also set a precedent in copyright law when in 1888 its author won a lawsuit against E. V. Seebohm over the rights to theatrical adaptations of the work.

Aa Bb Cc Dd Ee Ff Gg Hh Ii Jj Kk Ll Mm Nn Oo Pp Qq Rr Ss Tt Uu Vv Ww Xx Yy Zz

Comparative Fonts

Tempus Sans ITC– 12

Little Lord Fauntleroy is the first children's novel written by English playwright and author Frances Hodgson Burnett. It was originally published as a serial in the *St. Nicholas Magazine* between November 1885 and October 1886, then as a book by Scribner's in 1886. ¹The accompanying illustrations by Reginald Birch set fashion trends and *Little Lord Fauntleroy* also set a precedent in copyright law when in 1888 its author won a lawsuit against E. V. Seebohm over the rights to theatrical adaptations of the work.

Aa Bb Cc Dd Ee Ff Gg Hh Ii Jj Kk Ll Mm Nn Oo Pp Qq Rr Ss Tt Uu Vv Ww Xx Yy Zz

Comparative Fonts

Times New Roman 12

Little Lord Fauntleroy is the first children's novel written by English playwright and author Frances Hodgson Burnett. It was originally published as a serial in the *St. Nicholas Magazine* between November 1885 and October 1886, then as a book by Scribner's in 1886. ᴸThe accompanying illustrations by Reginald Birch set fashion trends and *Little Lord Fauntleroy* also set a precedent in copyright law when in 1888 its author won a lawsuit against E. V. Seebohm over the rights to theatrical adaptations of the work.

Aa Bb Cc Dd Ee Ff Gg Hh Ii Jj Kk Ll Mm Nn Oo Pp Qq Rr Ss Tt Uu Vv Ww Xx Yy Zz

Trebuchet MS- 12

Little Lord Fauntleroy is the first children's novel written by English playwright and author Frances Hodgson Burnett. It was originally published as a serial in the *St. Nicholas Magazine* between November 1885 and October 1886, then as a book by Scribner's in 1886. [The accompanying illustrations by Reginald Birch set fashion trends and *Little Lord Fauntleroy* also set a precedent in copyright law when in 1888 its author won a lawsuit against E. V. Seebohm over the rights to theatrical adaptations of the work.

Aa Bb Cc Dd Ee Ff Gg Hh Ii Jj Kk Ll Mm Nn Oo Pp Qq Rr Ss Tt Uu Vv Ww Xx Yy Zz

Comparative Fonts

Tw Cen MT

Little Lord Fauntleroy is the first children's novel written by English playwright and author Frances Hodgson Burnett. It was originally published as a serial in the *St. Nicholas Magazine* between November 1885 and October 1886, then as a book by Scribner's in 1886. [The accompanying illustrations by Reginald Birch set fashion trends and *Little Lord Fauntleroy* also set a precedent in copyright law when in 1888 its author won a lawsuit against E. V. Seebohm over the rights to theatrical adaptations of the work.

Aa Bb Cc Dd Ee Ff Gg Hh Ii Jj Kk Ll Mm Nn Oo Pp Qq Rr Ss Tt Uu Vv Ww Xx Yy Zz

Tw Cen MT Condensed Extra Bold 12

Little Lord Fauntleroy is the first children's novel written by English playwright and author Frances Hodgson Burnett. It was originally published as a serial in the *St. Nicholas Magazine* between November 1885 and October 1886, then as a book by Scribner's in 1886. The accompanying illustrations by Reginald Birch set fashion trends and *Little Lord Fauntleroy* also set a precedent in copyright law when in 1888 its author won a lawsuit against E. V. Seebohm over the rights to theatrical adaptations of the work.

Aa Bb Cc Dd Ee Ff Gg Hh Ii Jj Kk Ll Mm Nn Oo Pp Qq Rr Ss Tt Uu Vv Ww Xx Yy Zz

Comparative Fonts

Utsaah- 12

Little Lord Fauntleroy is the first children's novel written by English playwright and author Frances Hodgson Burnett. It was originally published as a serial in the *St. Nicholas Magazine* between November 1885 and October 1886, then as a book by Scribner's in 1886. [i]The accompanying illustrations by Reginald Birch set fashion trends and *Little Lord Fauntleroy* also set a precedent in copyright law when in 1888 its author won a lawsuit against E. V. Seebohm over the rights to theatrical adaptations of the work.

Aa Bb Cc Dd Ee Ff Gg Hh Ii Jj Kk Ll Mm Nn Oo Pp Qq Rr Ss Tt Uu Vv Ww Xx Yy Zz

Vani- 12

Little Lord Fauntleroy is the first children's novel written by English playwright and author Frances Hodgson Burnett. It was originally published as a serial in the *St. Nicholas Magazine* between November 1885 and October 1886, then as a book by Scribner's in 1886. ⌐The accompanying illustrations by Reginald Birch set fashion trends and *Little Lord Fauntleroy* also set a precedent in copyright law when in 1888 its author won a lawsuit against E. V. Seebohm over the rights to theatrical adaptations of the work.

Aa Bb Cc Dd Ee Ff Gg Hh Ii Jj Kk Ll Mm Nn Oo Pp Qq Rr Ss Tt Uu Vv Ww Xx Yy Zz

Comparative Fonts

Verdana- 12

Little Lord Fauntleroy is the first children's novel written by English playwright and author Frances Hodgson Burnett. It was originally published as a serial in the *St. Nicholas Magazine* between November 1885 and October 1886, then as a book by Scribner's in 1886. [The accompanying illustrations by Reginald Birch set fashion trends and *Little Lord Fauntleroy* also set a precedent in copyright law when in 1888 its author won a lawsuit against E. V. Seebohm over the rights to theatrical adaptations of the work.

Aa Bb Cc Dd Ee Ff Gg Hh Ii Jj Kk Ll Mm Nn Oo Pp Qq Rr Ss Tt Uu Vv Ww Xx Yy Zz

Viner Hand ITC 12

Little Lord Fauntleroy is the first children's novel written by English playwright and author Frances Hodgson Burnett. It was originally published as a serial in the *St. Nicholas Magazine* between November 1885 and October 1886, then as a book by Scribner's in 1886. [1]The accompanying illustrations by Reginald Birch set fashion trends and *Little Lord Fauntleroy* also set a precedent in copyright law when in 1888 its author won a lawsuit against E. V. Seebohm over the rights to theatrical adaptations of the work.

Aa Bb Cc Dd Ee Ff Gg Hh Ii Jj Kk Ll Mm Nn Oo Pp Qq Rr Ss Tt Uu Vv Ww Xx Yy Zz

Comparative Fonts

Vrinda– 12

Little Lord Fauntleroy is the first children's novel written by English playwright and author Frances Hodgson Burnett. It was originally published as a serial in the *St. Nicholas Magazine* between November 1885 and October 1886, then as a book by Scribner's in 1886. [The accompanying illustrations by Reginald Birch set fashion trends and *Little Lord Fauntleroy* also set a precedent in copyright law when in 1888 its author won a lawsuit against E. V. Seebohm over the rights to theatrical adaptations of the work.

Aa Bb Cc Dd Ee Ff Gg Hh Ii Jj Kk Ll Mm Nn Oo Pp Qq Rr Ss Tt Uu Vv Ww Xx Yy Zz

Comparative Fonts

Comparative Fonts

6

www.ingramcontent.com/pod-product-compliance
Lightning Source LLC
Chambersburg PA
CBHW051253050326
40689CB00007B/1174